AF259064

go within, or be without

Joy Alantis

Turning
f[OR]ty

If you have already turned 40-years-old
write about the lessons you learned about
yourself on your milestone birthday.

If you have not yet turned 40-years-old
write about who you intend to be when you
reach this milestone birthday.

Think about your belief systems in
contrast to who you are at your core
and your behavior.

Do they align?

OBJECTIVE

I choose.

Finding the [OR] in Forty

I pray that
you see me.

Joy Alantis

All the Queen's [ME]n

If you are in a relationship write down the joys and pains you have endured or are still working through with your partner.

If you are not in a relationship write down the joys and pains of your past relationships, romantic and platonic.

Think about your relationships in contrast to your relationship with your parents. What did they teach you about yourself versus what you have or want in your partner?

How are these experiences similar?

This also applies to those who have partnerships with wo[me]n.

OBJECTIVE

I learn to see myself in you.

Finding [ME] in Men

When I lost you I began to find me.

Joy Alantis

fami[LIAR]
Aick

If you are in a relationship, write about the moments that held you and your partner together because of your physical connection.

If you are not in a relationship write about the moments you relied upon sex to fill voids in your life to make you feel complete.

Think about your first encounter with sexuality. Was it freely explored or shamed? What did your experience teach you to believe about love and self-worth?

How do you reconcile the two?

Finding the [LIAR] in the Familiar

Put upon by
the poison of a
silent insecurity
I stand with you.

Joy Alantis

Gaining [CON]trol

If you are in a relationship write about how you may have intentionally or unintentionally sought control of your partner through manipulation.

If you are not in a relationship write about how you intentionally or unintentionally seek control of situations through manipulation.

Think about times you told a lie, big or small, to get what you wanted. Write about how you stage information for predictable responses?

How does this behavior serve your union?

Finding the [ICON] in Control

We stay balanced
[in the middle]
because every day is
a "wins" day for us

Joy Alantis

ill[US]ion

If you are in a relationship write about how you consistently lose yourself in your partner's needs and wants.

If you are not in a relationship write about how you continuously serve others before you serve yourself.

Think about times you have sacrificed to prove yourself as a worthy choice for your partner. Write about the people who taught you that depleting yourself was how you show love.

Is this your strength or weakness?

Finding [US] in the Illusion

Not only do I yearn for you, but I burn for you.

Joy Alantis

dys[FUN]ction

Write about the dynamics of your relationship between you and your father and you and members of your father's family. Be detailed.

Write about the dynamics of your relationship between you and your mother, and you and members of your mother's family. Be detailed.

Write about the dynamics of your relationship between you and your siblings, and you and your friends. Be detailed.

How are these relationships similar to your intimate relationships?

Finding [FUN] in dysfunction

It
[BE]gins
with me

Who [I am]

Write down how you describe yourself to others.

Why [I am]

Write down the reasons you believe
what you believe about yourself.

 What [I am]

Write down the things that make you, you.

I am great at...

I struggle with...

Things I want most...

Things I must heal / change...

Relation[SHIP]s

How do you feel in your relationships?

List the top 3 *common* behaviors of you and
your partner(s) during each relationship.

You

1) ....

2) ....

3) ....

Your
Partner(s)

1) ....

2) ....

3) ....

List 3 things you can do differently to change
the outcome of your relationship.

1)

2)

3)